D1527104

Diksha (initiation) is the seed of Kriya Yoga. Without initiation, Kriya will not bear fruit…

Copyright © 2017 by Rangin Mukherjee. All rights reserved. This book or any portion thereof may not be reproduced or used in any manner whatsoever without the express written permission of the publisher with the exception of short quotations used in conjunction with a book review.

First edition

Rangin Mukherjee
Kolkata INDIA

See www.originalkriya.com for more information about the author and the book.

Original Kriya Yoga
Step-by-Step Guide to Salvation
Vol. I - Essential Practices

Acknowledgements

The following people provided invaluable aid and advice on the compilation and publication of this book, including translation, correction, editing, promotion and final publication:

Mr. Chris Tar, Dr. James Glen Dening, Dr. (Mrs.) Christine Dening, Mr. Ennio Nimis, Mr. Jim Roberts, Mr. Babloo Mohanty, Mr. Sharath Jakob, Mr. D Gopal Suri, Mr. Samir Brijwasi, Mr. Sharath Jakob, Mr. Kevin Hoshang, Mr. Andre Vas

Revered Babaji Maharaj (Khitishwar Maharaj)

Revered Yogiraj Lahiri Mahasaya

My Param Gurudev Revered Paramahansa Pranabananda

Dedication

To my Guruji's lotus feet

Shri Gyanendra Nath Mukhopadhyay

(Shri Gyan Maharaj)

Table of Contents

Note from the author

Dear reader,

I have tried to write details about Kriya Yoga, which is somehow very difficult to explain in other languages. But, I have tried to explain as much as possible to at least give you an idea about Kriya Yoga, which is until now not correctly revealed. I would appreciate it very much if the readers would send me their feedback. I wish you all to enjoy this book, and make progress in Kriya Yoga and get salvation in the future, after getting initiation from a realized Guru. In Volume II of this book, I will provide a contact email for those who are looking for a Kriya Yoga Guru for initiation. If you have feedback on this book, you can reach me at originalkriyayoga@gmail.com

God Bless you all,

Rangin Mukherjee (Sri Mukherjee)

Introduction

At the request of many people, I have written this book on the "Original Kriya Yoga Techniques of Lahiri Mahasaya". I am not entirely sure whether such an act, of trying to express such a difficult subject in writing, is correct on my part or not. However, after talking to many Kriyabans (Kriya practitioners), I came to understand that what is given to them in the name of the original Kriya Yoga of Lahiri Mahasya is not at all Kriya Yoga. Many Kriyabans have adopted these processes and techniques and practiced them for many years without achieving any results. In some cases, even faithful practice for over 40 years has not yielded any result.

The Kriya techniques about which I am going to write are what I have received from my Guru Shri Shri Gyanendranath Mukhopadhyay. My Guru received it from His Guru Swami Pranabanandaji. Swami Pranabanandaji received this from the revered Lahiri Mahasaya. I have heard that Swami Pranabanada Giri was the main disciple of Lahiri Baba and I know my Guruji Shri Shri Gyanendranath Mukhopadhyay was the main disciple of Swami Pranabanandaji. This lineage is not affiliated with any organization which is why this Kriya Yoga is preserved in its original and unaltered form to this day. It is very difficult to say what will happen in the future if it falls in the hands of unauthorized, business-minded people. Many people have unnecessarily modified and complicated the simple techniques of this Kriya Yoga. My only aim in writing this book is to present the original essence of Kriya Yoga to you all. But be careful. It is dangerous to practice this by mere reading of a book without getting proper guidance from a Guru. This is why it is called "Gurumukhi Vidya" or "a lesson that has to be obtained directly from the mouth of the Guru". First of all, one should get initiation from a Sat Guru and only then start practicing this Kriya Yoga. Otherwise, it will not be fruitful.

Kriya practitioners who are practicing the initial stages, and have not yet entered Sushumna may find some portions of this book difficult to understand. As it is not possible to understand higher mathematics for a primary school student, advanced Kriya techniques will simply not make sense until you've mastered earlier stages. This book is written both for beginners as well as advanced Kriya practitioners. It will help the Kriya practitioner at all stages, and it can be used as a reference also. I will try to elaborate further in a second edition, due to be published sometime in 2017. Some portions of this book are taken from my short online book, but it is greatly expanded to include more detail and explanations. Some writings you may find repeated in this book to explain the technique more clearly.

Wonders of Original Kriya

We human beings are so ignorant that we spend most of the time of our lives searching for materialistic things which we cannot take with us and we spend very little time on the things which we will carry with us after death. We are running after many temporary things and spending so much energy for absolutely nothing. If we would have given so much labour for Kriya or God, we could have gotten salvation in one lifetime. This human tendency comes from ego or binding (Moha). This is the game of God. So, whatever time we have already wasted, let us not repent for that, but start Kriya immediately without wasting any more time. Even if we do not get success in this lifetime, we will again get this Kriya in our next life (if it is Original Kriya and not the fake one) and the Kriya of this life will be carried over to the next life. The effort spent does not get lost. That is why some achieve Samadhi in a few months, some yogis get Samadhi in few years and some get it immediately during initiation. This all happens due to work done in the previous life.

A poor farmer dreamt that he had become king, had a large kingdom with lots of ministers, a big army and a castle full of servants etc. In his dream he was seated in a throne made out of gold and precious stones, with royal dancers performing in front of him. He was very happy and had seven sons. Suddenly, his kingdom collapsed, his royal palace was drowned, and his seven princes each died one by one. At that very moment, the wife of the poor farmer called to wake him from his deep sleep and relayed news about the death of their only son, who was bitten by a snake. But the farmer isn't disturbed by the news. His wife thinks he must still be half asleep. His wife cried loudly and gave the

sad news again. He says "Yes, I heard you,
only I don't know for which tragedy I should
cry... Shall I cry for my big kingdom
collapsed and my seven princes dead, or
shall I cry for the death of my only son!?"

Both situations are dreams and we are so busy with this dream and so involved with this life that we forget to think about the truly valuable things in this world…

Why Does Man Want Salvation?

We do not know how many times we have taken birth and suffered from pain, disease, suffering from old age and finally the pain of death. The eternal cycle of the birth and death of the individual soul travels through different levels of existence and consciousness starting from the smallest virus/bacteria up to animals and then finally taking birth in the form of a human being. We forget the memories of our past life due to effect of the Veil as desired by God. Yogis can remember the experiences of past lives.

The world we live in is mortal because one who takes birth here will surely die one day. The day we take birth, our death sentence is signed. The Veil covers all this. Just as the criminal on death row worries more and more each day, and vows never to commit the crime again, so our death sentence is signed because we forget God and get entangled in this materialistic world through the effect of the Veil and through attachment.

By the effect of the Veil and attachment, we consider things to be our own which are actually not ours, while keeping away from us the one thing that actually *is* ours. It means we forget God and do not have the goal of being merged with Him. It's only when we face a problem in our life that we remember Him, and when the problem fades, we forget Him again.

We are constantly exposed to this materialistic world, starting from birth. We face tensions in every phase of our life, starting with childhood when we go to school and then in our professional lives, not to mention all the complications of marital life. For small, momentary materialistic pleasures we do so many things and chase after them. We don't spend time trying to find eternal bliss and joy. We fall prey to lifelong wrong habits and work to get joy for only short periods of time.

When there is strength in our body during youth, we feel ourselves to be very happy, and materialistic life looks like the recipe for correct living. At that time, we think that the rest of our life also will pass in the same fashion, but this is not the case. This materialistic life is only temporary. Nothing is permanent in this world. When the baby cries, the mother gives some toy so that the baby can play with it and it forgets the mother for some time. However, if the baby continues to cry, then the mother takes him/her in her lap. The same thing happens with us when we become satisfied with the materialistic world. Living life this way, we will never get the blessings of God and receive permanent joy and happiness.

When we age, our body slowly degenerates and different types of diseases and sufferings attack our body. Can we get the same enjoyment of youth while lying in a hospital bed with tubes passing through our mouth or nose and taking only saline as food? At last, when the time of death comes nearer and nearer, it is impossible for us to leave the attraction towards materialistic things like family, friends, money, house etc. And, this is only the mental side of the pain. Besides this, man gets bewildered at that time with bodily pain, breathing trouble etc. Man loses the ability to hear, see, touch and speak. Doctors, family members and friends watch helplessly. Man lies senselessly.

At the time of death, the results of all our accumulated deeds (whether good or bad) come as a vision and surround one. The condition of the next birth is decided based on whatever thought is fixed in the mind during the last breath. That is why the last breath is so important. Kriya Yoga (which is also called Raja Yoga or Bramha Vidya) is the only way to be free from these sufferings of birth & death, again and again which we invite by opting for momentary joy. Those who are still in the dark and are still satisfied with the materialistic joy can take the help of their consciousness and start practicing Kriya Yoga. With a change of their habits, one day they will surely be free from this cycle of life and death. So, it is not too late. Start from today. Kriya practice is never wasted. Even if the total Kriya is not completed in this birth, it will be surely completed in the next birth.

Even common man can attain the state of a great Sadhaka (Yogi) as a result of Sadhana (Kriya) carried out in several births. Eternal bliss (Bramhananda) can be attained by us.

6

Hence we should follow the path of such great people and practice as advised by them. But be careful about one thing when you advance on the path of Kriya Yoga. Whatever spiritual vision or feeling you get, by mistake also, you should never disclose to anybody other than your Guru. If you share this with others, it can only increase your ego, which is a direct obstacle to the goal of salvation. Many occult powers (Vibhuti) will come to you, but you should not accept those. If you accept these powers then you will be diverted from the spiritual path and your further progress will stop. All your spiritual Sadhana will have been in vain. All these powers are given by God only. God tests the Sadhaka with these to see whether Sadhaka really seeks God or occult powers. If you want these occult powers, you will earn name and fame in society; you will earn lots of money too. But, it will also lead to an increase in pride and arrogance and will ultimately lead you to the path of ruin. So, be careful. Otherwise you will spoil your state before and after death. Do your Sadhana behind closed doors. Nobody should be able to know what you are doing.

Why Practice Kriya Yoga?

Everything you see in this world is perishable! Nothing stays for long, including your body, youth, money and life itself. When a person is young and full of health, he thinks that life is excellent and enjoyable, but soon this dream ends... Health deteriorates, aging occurs, and health issues attack the body. Suddenly one sees the most dangerous moment in front of him/her - "the moment of Death", which is inevitable.

Once the king of Udaipur, Rajasthan in India asked Swamiji to give him some advice. Swami Pranabanandaji told the king, "The one thing you should remember, the greatest truth of all, is that you have to die one day. This is the best advice I can give you: The time of death is the worst time of anyone's life. On one side one suffers from pain and inability to breath, and on the other hand the emotional pain of leaving behind friends, relatives and all types of relationships. One goes into a dark world, where one suffers physically and mentally"

My purpose here is not to scare you but to show you the path to get freedom from all these sufferings which are happening with every birth you take! You yourself don't know how many times you came to this world, be it as parasite, different form of animal, bird, etc. It could be as many as 8 million births! Lord Sri Krishna said to Arjuna, "you yourself don't know how many births you have taken, but I know..." Someone asked the Buddha about his previous births and he said he remembered his last 500 births, one of which was as a rabbit and another as a deer.

We must remember that we come into this world with empty hands and we will leave this world with empty hands. Nobody will share the suffering of our death! Only our karma (our deeds) will go with us as samskaras (mind impressions) to our next life. So, we must be careful to not fall into the trap of Maya (binding), and try to do more good deeds in our life.

Even if we donate something out of charity, we must be careful that we are not donating to the wrong person.

If you give money to an alcoholic and with your money he drinks and in a state of intoxication commits a crime, you will have to share the sin that was done, because the donor's money was involved in it. If you donate to the right person, that money will come back to you many fold, and if not immediately, then surely in the next life. This is the reason why some are born into rich families and some into poor. To get rid of suffering the great yogis discovered Kriya yoga. By the correct practice of Kriya we get Mukti (Salvation), we go beyond suffering, and ultimately dissolve with the Almighty, becoming free from the cycle of birth and death. Kriya Yoga is the simplest, fastest and easiest way to liberate yourself. If you practice according to the instructions, you are bound to get Salvation in this or the next life.

Unfortunately, some people have turned this into something completely different due to improper guidance and miscommunication between Guru and disciple. Discussing anything further about altered Kriya is waste of precious time.

Some Points to Remember

- A Kriya Practitioner should practice at least 2 times a day i.e. mornings and evenings 2 hours each time in the beginning and 3 hours after some advancement.

- Kriya should be practised very comfortably without rushing to complete the Kriya.
- A Kriya practitioner should not eat anything 4 to 6 hours prior to practising Kriya.
- During Kriya practice one should sit on a pure woollen blanket with pure silk on it.
- No portion of the body should touch the floor.
- Sitting posture should be perfect, without any movement of any parts of the body.
- Mental eyes should be fixed in the centre of the eyebrows or Agna chakra without straining the physical eyes.
- Chant" OM" 6 times during inhalation and 6 times during exhalation; simultaneously mind should be fixed in Agna chakra.
- Siddhasan is the best asana for Kriya practice.
- Only satvik foods should be taken. Food is very important factor for Kriya practitioners. No eggs, meats etc. Fish, vegetables, fruits are allowed.
- Too much or too little of anything is no good for a Kriya practitioner: eating, working, walking, sleeping, drinking too hot or too cold, too spicy etc.
- Six or Six and half hours of sleep is enough.
- Too much T.V watching, chatting, reading different books, gossiping is forbidden.
- Lady companions are not acceptable.
- After a little advancement, celibacy has to be maintained.
- Always practice Kriya inside a dark room.
- Never talk about any visions, powers or any other experience you get.
- Keep this technique a total secret, otherwise a Kriya practitioner will lose the grace of God and will be placed in the dark world again.

- Without initiation, a Kriya practitioner will never succeed. First, a Kriya practitioner should take Kriya initiation from a realised Guru and then should practice Kriya Yoga. Getting initiation from a fake Guru is the same as wasting time.
- A person can be judged by lifting their hands. If the hands of a person are found to be heavy when lifting their hands, then it means he/she is not fit for practicing Kriya yoga. A practitioner's hands should be light in weight and if they are found to be light weight they are fit to Kriya practice.
- The flow of urine of a materialistic person goes to the left side and the flow of urine of a yoga practitioner goes to the right side.
- A Kriya Practitioner should live like a blind, deaf & dumb person i.e. not seeing too much things, not hearing too much gossip and not talking unnecessarily.
- The best time to practice Kriya for advanced student is from 9:30 evening to 4:30 morning. At that time, many realised Yogis travel with their astral body and if they find someone practising Kriya at that time, they bless them.
- Until we pierce Agna chakra, Pranayam is the only Kriya (Sadhana) we need to practice. The speed of our development in Kriya yoga depends on perfect Pranayama.
- Whether we do good deeds or bad deeds during our lives, we have to take birth to get the results of all the deeds which we have done. Doing any deed whether good or bad comes from the restlessness of the mind. The only way to get rid of all the deeds and their results is the calmness of mind or Samadhi where no deeds exist.
- Doing perfect Kriya with subtle breath changes the entire character of a person.

- Many Kriya practitioners may wonder how it is possible to enter Brahmanadi. We enter with the astral body only.
- During Kriya, we have to get rid of all egos and do not try to control your breathing. Always practice kriya by breathing normally in the beginning, without using any force on breath. Keep your mind always fixed on Agna chakra without squinting or straining your eyes throughout your practice.
- Before starting Kriya, take time to get rid of all kind of thoughts - the mind should be clear and free of thoughts and not filled with commitments & distractions.
- We should constantly remind ourselves that nothing belongs to us and we ourselves belong only to ourselves
- We should practice Kriya very seriously and honestly with devotion towards God. Do not forget that God is watching us 24*7, his eyes are always open and never blink. He is inside Kutastha. One cannot hide anything from him.
- If your house belongs to you, your property belongs to you, your wife or husband or children and everything belong to you, then at the time of death, why can't you take them with you? You came to this world empty handed and you will leave this world empty handed. Nothing belongs to you and you belong to nobody, so forget uttering these words. Even this body doesn't belong to you. This is nothing but ego which is given to us by God in order to preserve his creation.

Yogic Powers (Yoga Siddhis)

In Kriya yoga, the miracle power starts coming after entering Sushumna. Every chakra right from "Muladhar" is ruled by a particular God & Goddess. When a kriya practitioner enters these chakras, the rulling God of that particular chakra appears & they offer different types of powers (siddhis) to judge the Kriya practitioner's greed towards having these powers. If a Kriya practitioner falls into these traps, he will definitely get those powers which will help him to earn name, fame & money. But ultimately he will lose the grace of god and will fail to reach his target of salvation. Therefore strictly he should avoid those attractive powers and request the rulling god to open the door and allow him to move further towards the next chakra. This way the ruling god will be pleased, bless the Kriya practitioner, open the door, and guide him to the next chakra. As the Kriya Practitioner pierces one by one each of the chakras, he will get various attractive powers. But he should reject all these powers to reach his target. One should keep in mind these powers are temporary. They will leave the Kriya practitioner at the time of death and he will have to leave this world empty handed with lot of bad deeds also.

That is why my strong advice is not to accept any power, no matter how much it could be attractive. Then a Kriya practitioner will get salvation. Like this, God wants to see whether a Kriya practitioner is seeking him or seeking those powers. If you seek powers you will not get him and if you seek him only you must avoid accepting those powers.

A Kriya practitioner after getting salvation can use any type of powers. At that time nothing can harm him, but not before getting salvation.

If you have a thirst for getting those powers then don't practice Kriya Yoga. You will spoil your life. A person with a crooked mind can never succeed in Kriya Yoga. God is simple minded and only a simple minded person can only succeed in Kriya Yoga.

Gurutav Siddhi:
The person who is full of knowledge and wisdom and has the capacity to transmit it is known as guru and bhagawan sri krishna is known as jagatguru, the guru of this entire universe.

Purna purushatva Siddhi:
This means someone who is vigorous and full of virtues. Sri Krishna had all virtues from his birth due to which he killed all the demons and reestablished dharma.

Iccha mrityu Siddhi:
Acquiring this siddhi, the yogi becomes the winner of time. Time loses its effect on them. They can leave their body and get a new one at their will.

Anurmi Siddhi:
The word anurmi means the one who is beyond hunger, thirst, heat, cold, good and bad. Thus, acquiring this, one becomes free of everything above.

Vaak Siddhi:
This siddhi gives the yogi the complete power over his words. Attainment of this siddhi ensures that no word of yogi

is wasted, what they say or speak will be done, be it a blessing or a curse.

Divya Drishti Siddhi:
The siddhi of clairvoyance or foresight, this enables the yogi to see the past, present and future of anyone at their will.

Dura Sravana siddhi:
This siddhi gives yogis the power to hear once again any conversations of the past at their will in the present moment.

Jalagaman Siddhi:
Attaining this siddhi the yogi is able to walk on water just like walking on earth.

Vayugaman Siddhi:
This siddhi gives the ability to transform the body into very subtle form and travel from one dimension to others in no time.

Adrishya karan Siddhi:
Helps in transforming the physical body to the Astral body for being invisible and they can then be invisible as long as one wishes.

Vishoka Siddhi:
This is the power to transform one into any form, to choose what you want to look like at will.

Devkriyanudarshana Siddhi:

With a complete understanding of this siddhi one is able to gain the confidence of devas and ask them for help in any event.

Kayakalp Siddhi:
To change this body and keep it forever young and full of energy is kayakalp. Attaining this a yogi never ages. (for example, Shree Babaji Maharaj)

Sammohan Siddhi:
Sammohan means to make anyone do your will! Having this siddhi, a yogi can control not only human minds but birds, animals and nature.

Importance of Kriya Initiation

In Kriya Yoga, mass initiation is strictly forbidden. Kriya Yoga initiation should be done face to face between the Guru and the disciple, in a dark room, behind closed doors. No one else should be present. During initiation, the duty of the guru is to open the third eye or divine eye, transfer the power of the lineage, and explain to the disciple the correct practice of Kriya Yoga.

Mass initiation is not at all initiation. It is only a joke. With mass initiation, a disciple can never progress or achieve anything, even with a lifetime of practice. Without opening the third eye, one can never experience anything in the divine world. Without the two physical eyes, we would not be able to see in the materialistic world. Similarly, without our divine eye or third eye being opened, we cannot see anything in the inner world or divine world. We are as a blind person in the divine world. That is why there is a sanskrit sloka showing respect to the Guru, as written hereunder:

Akhanda mandalākāram
vyāptam yena charācharam
Tat padam darshitam yena
tasmai shri gurave namah.

I bow to that Guru, who shows the state of that perfectly round Kutastha pervading the indivisible form of the universe, penetrating everything, be it mobile or immobile.

Agnāna timirāndhasya gnānānjana shalākakayā
Chakshurnmilitam yena tasmai shri gurave namah

I bow to that Guru who with the help of the collyrium of knowledge dispels the blind folding darkness of ignorance, and opens my inner eyes.

Difference Between Teacher and Guru

Teachers give us the materialistic knowledge but from Sat Guru we get spiritual wisdom which liberates us. Materialistic knowledge goes away after death whereas spiritual knowledge stays with us until we are liberated from the cycle of life and death. Therefore, in Hinduism, the Sat guru is compared with God because through Guru, the disciple gets the blessing of God. In the case of a fake guru, what we get is frustration, loss of interest, depression and a waste of time!

There are three types of doctors you can go to see - one will take a quick look, give you a prescription, and send you on your way. The next type will spend lots of time with you to make sure they really understand the condition before prescribing medicine or a course of action. The third and best type will not only spend the time to make sure they have the right diagnosis, but they will follow up regularly to make sure you are taking their advice, and that your condition is improving. So it is with gurus. The best gurus will not only take the time to get to know you and give you what you best need, they will ask to see your methods, and constantly make sure that you're not wasting your time doing the wrong thing.

Duty of Guru - Duty of Disciple

The duty of Guru is to plant the seed and the duty of the disciple is to take care of the seed so that tree grows properly and in the end yield fruit. It means the Guru will initiate the disciple, and explain to them how to navigate the path. The duty of the disciple is to obey the Guru`s instructions sincerely, and ultimately get Salvation.

Diksha (initiation) is the most important aspect of Sadhana. It is like the second birth of Sadhak in the spiritual world. Without Diksha or initiation from a Sat Guru, the Kriyas discussed here simply hold no power.

Diksha is like a seed and daily Sadhana of these Kriyas is the water. Both Diksha and Sadhana work together for spiritual growth of the practitioner. Initiation is not just revealing the techniques of Kriya. There is more to it than that. It is the transfer of a spark of light from one soul to another, and connects the disciple with the lineage of Sri Lahiri Baba, Swami Pranabananda Giri, and Sri Gyanendra Nath Baba. This transfer activates the sleeping divine energy inside the practitioner and pushes his/her consciousness towards a more positive and sattvic state. Diksha/Initiation is a very secret affair between Guru and disciple. It establishes an unbreakable bond between Guru and disciple. Without diksha sadhana is useless..

Your biological father is responsible for helping to bring you into the material world, but the Sat Guru becomes your spiritual father, birthing you into the spiritual world.

I have seen that after taking Kriya initiation many people start practising Kriya for a few months with full zeal and enthusiasm. But when initially they do not get any spiritual feeling or vision,
they lose interest, leave Kriya practice, and start living in the usual worldly way. But they should remember that for getting success in any work, perseverance and patience are

required. One cannot attain spiritual enlightenment by mere magic.

That is why Lord Sri Krishna instructed in "Srimad Bhagavad Gita" to do work without any attachment to its result (Nishkam Karma). What is this "Nishkam Karma"? It means to practice Kriya correctly as per the advice of Guru without worrying for the result. Result will surely come but at first perseverance, patience and faith are required. By practicing in this way, Kriya in the six Chakras will end (by piercing the Agna chakra) and Kriya of devotion (Bhakti) and knowledge (Gyana) will start in the Sahasrasar.

Kriya Yoga Sadhana (Practice)

There are eight steps in Yoga Sadhana: Controlling of the senses (Yama), strict discipline (Niyama), correct posture (Asana), control of Life-forces (Pranayam), withdrawing from the outer senses (Pratyahar), fixing mind to a particular object or thought (Dharana), and diving deep inside to almost merge into Eternal Truth (Dhyana). Then the Sadhaka merges with the Eternal Truth and becomes the one (Samadhi). Though these steps are common in both Kriya Yoga and Raja Yoga, there are some differences too. There are some mudras and special techniques included in Kriya Yoga for the benefit of Kriya practice. From the Patrabali (Garland of Letters) of Lahiri Mahasaya, we find that he has written to one of his disciples that "Everything is achievable with First Kriya. Parabastha(Samadhi) and Divine intoxication, everything is there in First Kriya". My Guruji also said that one can attain Samadhi with First Kriya only.

Nowadays some people have started doing business in India and West in the name of Kriya Yoga (and in the name of Original Kriya Yoga too) and to show their superiority over others, they have added many unnecessary and difficult techniques to this simple Kriya Yoga. So, I request the readers not to fall into such business traps. First Kriya includes:

- Asana (Sitting in correct posture)
- Pranayam (Kriya for control of Life-force)
- Yonimudra
- Mahamudra
- Parabastha (Pratyahar- withdrawal of mind from outer senses).

Parabastha eventually deepens into the stages of Dharana, Dhyana and Samadhi. Everything comes automatically. The only requirement is love towards God, devotion and practicing Kriya correctly. This is the original Kriya given by Yogiraj Shymacharan Lahiri Mahasaya.

Khechari Mudra

Please note that if a kriya practitioner cannot perform khechari mudra, there is nothing to worry about. Khechari mudra can definitely help to concentrate in the kutastha but it is not absolutely necessary. During Kriya, just touch your tongue at the upper palate (just beyond the teeth) of your mouth, so that saliva during advanced kriya will not come out, just like the position of the tongue during sleeping. There are lots of realised yogis in India, who haven't practiced khechari mudra, nor they have heard about khecharii mudra. For example Swami Vivekananda didn't know about khechari mudra. My Guruji also told me that khechari mudra is not necessary.

Mystery of Kriya Yoga

The mystery of Kriya Yoga lies on the basis of ***crossing the boundary of mind and intellect by watching the Life-force*** (Prana) and the process of merging the individual spirit (Jivatma) into the Eternal Spirit (Paramatma). So, first one has to practice Kriya using the five energy centres in the spine (five Chakras). Then one pierces the chakras one by one and at last pierces the Agna chakra. Piercing Agna chakra ends Kriya practice in the six energy centres. After that, Kriya starts in the field of intellect (Buddhi Kshetra) and in the field of Eternity (Parama Kshetra).

It is important to clearly understand the relation between the Life-force (Prana), mind (Mana), intellect (Buddhi), individual spirit (Jivatma) and the eternal spirit (Parmatma). If breathing becomes frequent and uncontrolled, mind becomes restless and on the other-hand, if mind becomes restless, breathing becomes frequent and uncontrolled. Both mind and breathing are inter-dependent. As breathing is gross in nature (Sthula in Sanskrit) and mind is subtle (Sukshma in

Sanskrit), we work to control the breath first because controlling the gross is easier than controlling the subtle. That is why it is required to control breathing first with the help of Pranayam, and slowly it will become subtle.

Moreover, the concept of the relation and difference between breathing, Life-force (Prana) and mind should be clear. Breathing is controlled by Life-force; however it cannot be termed *directly* as Life-force. The force or the energy which helps bring air inside the body during the inbreath and the outflow of air from the body during the outbreath is nothing but the Life-force or Prana. This Life-force is distributed all over the body and all the internal organs are controlled by this Life-force. That is why the internal organs stop working in the absence of Life-force and then it is declared as a dead body. Life force can be compared with electricity by which all our body organs function.

In simple language, it can be explained in this way: at first by controlling the breath, breath should be converted from subtle to extremely subtle. **The state of this extremely subtle breathing is the same as the Life-force.** And the state of subtle Life-force is mind. State of subtle mind is intellect. The state of subtle intellect is individual spirit (Jivatma) and the state of extremely subtle individual spirit is universal spirit (Parmatma).

As the Life-force becomes more & more subtle, the Prana Vayu (breathing) becomes extremely subtle; it will not flow through the nose any longer, and will instead move inside the body through Sushumna. In this condition of Kumbhak where the breath no longer flows through the nose, the

Prana or Life-force moves in Sushumna and mind will slowly merge into Life-force and will start moving together. With this Life-force and mind, it is required to pierce the six chakras. After piercing Agna Chakra, it is seen that there is no relation between mind and Life-force. Then mind becomes even more subtle and merges with intellect and Kriya starts in the space of intellect. After completion of Kriya in the space of intellect, it becomes even more subtle and merges into individual spirit (Jivatma). At that time it is required to take the individual spirit into the space of universal eternal spirit (Paramatma) and merge the Jivatma in Paramatma. At the end it is required to pierce the Mula chakra and submerge in formless Brahma (Nirguna Brahma) . This is called the stage of Brahmalin or Salvation.

Ashtanga (8-fold) Yoga

As described earlier, there are eight steps common to Kriya Yoga and Raja Yoga. They are the controlling of senses (Yama), strict discipline (Niyama), correct posture (Asana), control of Life-force (Pranayam), withdrawing from outer senses (Pratyahar), fixing mind to a particular object or thought (Dharana), diving deep inside to almost merge into Eternal Truth (Dhyana) and then Sadhaka and the Eternal Truth become one (Samadhi). The first five steps i.e Yama, Niyama, Asana, Pranayam & Pratyahar are included in Karma Yoga (Yoga of action). Dharana, Dhyana, and Samadhi are Kriyas done in the field of intellect (Buddhi) and divinity (Paramakhetra). So, they are the Kriyas of devotion and knowledge or Kriyas done in Sahasrasar.

Yama

The first important thing is food. If the food eaten by Sadhaka is not Sattvic in nature, then there is no chance of spiritual improvement, because if the body becomes restless, mind will also become restless. If we eat sugar, we experience the sensation of sweetness. On the other hand, when we eat tamarind, we experience the sensation of sourness. So, it is clear that different types of food activate different taste sensations in our body. Likewise, different kinds of food have different qualities and nutritional value. One type of food is rich in Vitamin-B and another type may be rich in Vitamin C, etc. Similarly, different types of food affect our mind differently.

Following are examples of Sattvic food (for the benefit of English readers, it is worth mentioning here that English translations of some of the vegetables are not available): Pointed gourd (Parwal in Hindi or Patal in Bengali), saak (leafy vegetables), Chana dal, green gram dal (moong dal), split red gram (Tuvar dal/Arhar dal), carbohydrates (Sarkara), milk, dense milk (Kheer), ghee, fruits etc. Fruits & Vegetables are considered to be Sattvic. Those who are used to taking non-vegetarian food can eat small fish. Following are examples of Rajashik foods, which are to be avoided: egg, chicken/mutton, onion, garlic, mustard, asafoetida (Hing) etc. These foods create restlessness in body and mind and destroy the calmness, so these should be avoided. If these foods are consumed, it will drop a curtain over the spiritual eye (Abaran or Veil) or increase diversion/deflection (Bikshep). Examples of Tamasik foods (which creates Tamogun in the body) are: stored foods prepared earlier, food that's too sour, too hot or too cold. These foods create Tamogun in the body. It creates laziness, sleepiness and lack of enthusiasm in the body and evil thoughts.

Suppose a sadhak experiences that he/she is rapidly progressing in the Kriya path and suddenly eats two eggs. He/she will feel that his/her mind is disturbed, a veil will cover the Spiritual eye and the whole Kriya will be disturbed for 7-10 days. So, one should be careful about food during Kriya Practice.

Besides these, reading spiritual books, company of spiritual people, spiritual discussion, and honest behaviour also should be practiced. One should read The Gita every day. Participating in discussion about others & criticising others is to be strictly avoided. Too much gossip is also a distraction for the mind. One should not be too dependent on others. Gossiping or involving oneself in debate is not desired. One should not do excessive hard work (to the point of exhaustion). Watching television or movies is to be avoided. On the whole one should be blind, deaf & dumb. It means one should not see anything wrong, should not speak anything wrong or hear anything wrong. It may be difficult, but it's possible. Besides these celibacy (Brahmacharya) is also important. Otherwise, one will not be able to perceive the subtle spiritual feelings of the inner world.

One cannot progress much in the path of Yoga without becoming celibate. But some people initially feel depressed at the beginning while observing celibacy. For that reason, sexual practices should be gradually decreased. It should be totally stopped after entering Sushumna.

One should not eat until the stomach is full with food. It means one should eat up to the point when there is still some empty space left in the stomach. (One should stop eating food while some hunger still remains). Pranayam will not manifest to the persons who eat excess food. One should not practice Kriya within 5-6 hours of taking a meal. If one follows these disciplines, he can rapidly progress on the spiritual path. At the beginning one may feel depressed (this state of Sadhaka is described in the first chapter of Sri Bhagawata Gita: Vishada Yoga, but when one starts feeling the spiritual bliss, the worldly joy will become insignificant. Materialistic enjoyment is only 1/16th that of Divine Joy.

Generally it is seen that things which are favourites for materialistic enjoyment are detrimental for the spiritual path. Your spiritual striving will be tested by God in this manner - all materialistic enjoyable things will be placed before your eyes but if you try to play with those, you have to pay heavily on the path of spirituality. For this reason, self-control is a must. All the lust for materialistic enjoyment gets generated out of bodily attachment. All these are a play of the veil.

In this world, all the relations are based on a give and take policy, and it's the same with God. Everything belongs to God, so what will you give him? God demands respect, devotion and separation of our mind from worldly matters. In return he gives us Divine knowledge and Salvation.

Niyama (Discipline)

Everyday Kriya should be practiced at the same time and for the same duration. If one day, I get some joy in doing Kriya, and that day I do more Kriya, and then another day I am not getting any joy out of Kriya so I do less Kriya - this inconsistent way of practicing will be of no help. Everyday Kriya should be practiced following strict discipline. As time passes, the duration of Kriya practice will increase automatically. The best time to practice Kriya is between 9.30 PM and 4.30 AM, while sleeping for 3 hours in the afternoon, after taking lunch. One who practices Kriya during this time experiences many blessings because at that time lot of realised Yogis travel with the astral body and if they find someone practicing Kriya, they bless them. When your practice duration naturally lengthens, practicing continuously at this time is equivalent to practicing Kriya for 24 hours. Beginners should practice Kriya during early morning and in the evening, 2-3 hours before sunrise, and 2-3 hours after sunset.

The Number of Pranayams should be fixed every day during Kriya practice. For example, if you fix 108 times of Pranayam, the same number of Pranayams should be practiced every day. If today you are feeling spiritually motivated and practice Kriya for a long time, and another day you feel depressed and practice Kriya for a shorter time, this is not the way Kriya should be practiced. It is generally observed that for those who practice 108 Pranayams every day at the same time, upon reaching 70 to 80 Pranayams, the mind becomes calm. This is the effect of practicing Pranayam at a fixed time with a fixed number of Pranayams.

Kriya should be practiced without any worry in the mind. It will help with rapid progress in the Kriya path. For the fastest development, Kriya should be practiced at least twice a day in the beginning. If it's not possible, once every day is absolutely necessary. If one practices Kriya in the same time every day, he will notice that during that time of the day mind will become calm automatically. At advance stages one can practice Kriya whenever he likes and for any duration because at this stage the mind and Prana are under control of Sadhaka. The biggest enemy of Kriya practice is noise. One should practice Kriya in a calm & quiet atmosphere in a dark room.

Note : YAMA and NIYAMA are the foundation of a Yogi. Without maintaining YAMA and NIYAMA one can not succeed in Yoga.

Asana

Now let us discuss about asana (Posture for sitting in Sadhana). There are many varieties. But for Kriya practice Siddhasan or Swastikasan is the best and easy.

After sitting in asana, one should first inhale fully to expand the chest, and then maintain this posture of an expanded chest while doing pranayama. The arms and wrists should be straight out, with the wrists resting on the knees. Posture or asana should be in the state of "Samakaya Siragriba":

sama means in the same straight line, kaya means body, sira means head and griba means shoulders. It means the spine and the head should be placed in the same straight line. The chin should come slightly down towards throat by tilting the head down. Now it should be practiced to make the body totally still because unless the body becomes totally still, it is not possible to practice the Pranayam following the actual procedure. The sitting cushion should be like this: first cushion should be made out of Kusha grass, above that a wool blanket should be placed and on the top silk cloth to be placed. [Nowadays getting Kushasan may be difficult. Alternatively, one can make the sitting cushion with a pure white or plain coloured woollen blanket and a good quality silk cloth placed above that].

During Kriya practice one should be careful that no part of the body should touch the ground. Otherwise ground will absorb the spiritual energy generated out of Kriya practice. This includes keeping the silk on the wool blanket, and not touching the ground or floor. During Kriya practice one should be careful that the mastak granthi (it is physically located in medulla oblongata) and Agna chakra form a line that is parallel to ground. If during Kriya practice it is noticed that medulla oblongata has come down and Agna chakra has gone up, it indicates that mind is not there in Agna chakra but roaming in worldly thoughts. So during Kriya practice one should be careful that medulla oblongata and the centre of Agna chakra should form a straight line parallel to the ground.

Pranayam

Now let us discuss about the principle part of Sadhana that is Pranayam. There are two main hindrances in Sadhana. One is Abaran (a curtain or veil on the spiritual eye) and the other is diversion or deflection (bikshep). Abaran covers God in the similar fashion of dark clouds covering the sun. The sun is always there but when dark clouds cover the sun, it looks like there is no sun. Similarly, God is always there in Kutastha but due to the effect of Abaran, we are not able to perceive him always. Bikshep is where one tries to keep mind on the place where God is, but it gets deflected from there. By practicing Pranayam and following strict discipline of Yama & Niyama, this Abaran (veil on spiritual eye) slowly vanishes and Bikshep gets removed.

Because of this Abaran, when we close our eyes, we see total darkness. The inner sky will glow with more and more light as the veil of Abaran vanishes and we reach closer to God. To defeat this Abaran & Bikshep is the most important stage of Sadhana.

Though there are many varieties of Pranayam, the natural Pranayam which one gets from birth (Sahaja Pranayam) is the best Pranayam . This Pranayam was given by Lord Sri Krishna to his dearest disciple Arjuna. In this Pranayam, in the beginning, Pranab means to remember at every chakra the mantra (OM) and should be done with natural inhalation and exhalation. This means mentally chanting Om six times on the (natural) inbreath, and mentally chanting Om six times again on the (natural) outbreath. Mind and inner vision should be fixed at Kutastha which means at the centre point of Agna chakra. Agna chakra is located at the point between the eyebrows. In the beginning, it is very difficult to locate the centre point of Agna Chakra or Kutastha, which is why focus should be kept at the centre of the eyebrows and attention should be kept at the centre of any figures or shapes that appear there, in the inner vision (this is all with the eyes closed). **The centre of Agna Chakra is aligned / connected with the centre of all the other five chakras.** That's how we navigate all six chakras while focusing only on the centre of Agna chakra. This should be practiced without straining the eyes, and eventually vision will be automatically fixed at the centre point. Mind should not get diverted from this point. The tendency of mind will be to get diverted but again & again it should be pulled back and fixed at the point between eyebrows. With this, mind and Prana will move together at the point between the eyebrows. This is described by my Revered Guruji as keeping the mind with Prana or Life-force. This is the Kriya of six chakras. In the beginning, no force should be applied on breathing. In the beginning, the nadis / veins in the body remain blocked with bile, mucus & air. If force is applied in this condition, it may create many diseases. It will also hamper the spiritual advancement. In the beginning, as the nadis are cleaned, they simultaneously become filled with Prana. When they are fully cleaned, the body will become filled with Prana. In this way, the internal light will increase, and you will be able to see past/present/future.

Like this, Pranayam should be practiced day after day, month after month, year after year. One should not lose patience. That is why Thakur Ramakrishna said (Thakur literally means God – a Godly person) "the one who keeps patience survives but the one who loses patience gets destroyed". After practicing Pranayam for a long time like this, Pranayam eventually becomes subtle and then extremely subtle. One day mind will surely become fixed at the point between the eyebrows withoiut deflection, but until that time one should go on practicing Kriya in this way. When the mind becomes stable at the point between the eyebrows, the breathing will become extremely subtle. This is when force should be applied on the breathing during Kriya Pranayam. At that time, an overwhelming joy will fill the mind and the feeling will come that I have never experienced such joy earlier. Kriya should be practiced in this way until the lower part of Kutastha is crossed. Once the mind goes above Agna chakra, the Kriya of six chakras ends. Then mind and Life-force become stable, and by an unknown force (force or grace of God), the Kutastha is pierced and the mind and the Life-force rises to Sahasrasar. The same is being hinted at in the Bible by Jesus Christ: "Ask and it will be given to you; seek and you will find; knock and the door will be opened to you." [Matthew 7.7]. Here Jesus is not talking about a wooden door. This is the door of Kutastha. With Kriya Pranayam, the Sadhaka everyday knocks at the center doors of the six chakras and opens them one by one and reaches the center of Agna Chakra. The center of Agna Chakra or Kutastha can be opened with the Kripa (blessings) of God only. He sees that the Sadhaka has reached near to him, so He opens the door of Agna Chakra and brings the Sadhaka to Sahasrasar. Before piercing Kutastha, the Sadhaka keeps his focus on the east side of the body and after piercing Kutastha, he keeps his focus on the west side of the body. (The Front of the body is east, back is west.)

After practicing Kriya Pranayams and mudras (Jyoti mudra is mahamudra), one should not immediately get up. One should sit for some times focusing at the Kutastha and fixing the mind there. This is called parabastha, or the Kriya of Pratyahar or Kriya for withdrawing from the outer senses. This is meditation. During any part of kriya practice when one feels the divine intoxication or ecstasy, no Kriya should be practiced. When mind becomes fixed at Kutastha, one will be filled with Divine intoxication. One forgets himself in this condition and feels that he/she was in a state of total bliss but unable to remember that state exactly. He/She will not feel any desire to open the eyes, feels difficulty in talking and doesn't want to hear anything. He/She does not feel hungry or thirsty. While walking too steps will not be proper due to this state of Divine intoxication. After this stage Dharana, Dhyana and Samadhi Kriya can be perceived automatically at Sahasrasar.

Controlling the movement of Prana (Life force)

Imagine the Prana (life force) is a river flowing with great speed. If we dig canals by the side of the main stream of the river, then some of the water will start flowing through canals and the speed of the main river force will start slowing down. In this way, we can divert our Prana to move through different channels (Nadis) of the body. Then the flow of Prana can be controlled. This technique is to be applied in 2nd Kriya only, and just like this in 2nd kriya we have to force Prana (life force) to travel through different channels of our body. This way we can get many different powers, which help us to pierce different chakras and then fully gain control over Prana. Without controlling Prana, we will be not able to practice higher Kriyas. The main object of Pranayam is to get control over Prana.This is one of the most important aspect of Kriya Yoga.

Meditation (Dharana, Dyana, Samadhi)

Pratyahar (First stage of Meditation/ or Parabastha) After Pranayam, practice Yoni Mudra and Mahamudra. Then, as discussed above, sit silently, with the eyes closed, watching the centre of eye brows (Agna chakra) without chanting **'OM',** and sit in this way for 15-20 minutes in the beginning. Gradually, the duration to sit like this will increase automatically. One should only watch the centre of Agna chakra. Mind will get diverted again and again. One should repeatedly bring the mind back to the centre of Agna chakra. In this way, you will find that the mind is gradually getting settled and fixed at the centre of Agna Chakra. Your only task is to watch what is happening in Agna chakra. Eventually, with more and more practice, body awareness will cease and intoxication will come. After piercing Agna Chakra, you will do Dharana, as below:

A. **Dharana (2nd stage of Meditation):** This stage comes to the Sadhak after piercing Agna Chakra to the lower part of Sahasrasar chakra. In this stage, you will be able to concentrate deeper and get higher consciousness and hold your mind or concentrate on a particular object.

B. **Dhyana (3rd stage of Meditation):** This stage happens in the centre of Sahasrasar chakra. It is extremely deep Meditation and one starts getting extreme knowledge.

C. **Samadhi:** Here one forgets his identity and gets immersed in total bliss. At this stage, mind and intellect are lost and the individual soul becomes merged into the universal soul.

The time of death is the worst time of our life. All that we have sacrificed and achieved in Kriya Yoga is for this moment. The results of all the previously accumulated deeds (good or bad) appear as a vision at the time of death. During the last breath, one who has practiced Kriya yoga seriously and perfectly throughout his life should only concentrate in Kutastha and mentally chant Pranab **(Om).** In this way, by piercing Kutastha with the grace of God and destroying all the veils, one goes to Sahasrasar Chakra and gets Salvation by which you avoid the pain of death. At that very moment, neither the pain of death nor bindings to the world can touch you.

The Secret of "OM"

Om is the divine language of God. When repeated in a specific way, it creates vibrations that calm the mind and thoughts and bring one closer to the Almighty. Chanting **OM** during Pranayama has the power to activate all the Chakras. Before the Universe existed, only this sound was there. That is why **"OM"** is called the language of God or God himself. While doing Kriya, the japa of Om in the centre of each chakra is very important. The japa activates the chakras. Practicing Pranayam without chanting "OM" is like a breathing exercise only. It will not result in any spiritual development. Without japa, the Kriya becomes Tamasik and Kriya Yoga becomes fruitless.

I am not saying these things in order to criticize other methods of Kriya, but to show you the simplest, best and fastest way to reach and travel through Sushumna. In whatever way you do yoga (union with God) always remember that we have to travel through Sushumna to reach Almighty to get salvation, because Sushumna is the final route to God. Without entering Sushumna you cannot get Salvation. So why should we unnecessarily choose a difficult path to reach Sushumna, when there is such an easy process to enter? God is very simple, so he created a simple process to reach him. When there is a straight highway to reach him quickly, why should we go through small lanes and roads to reach him?

Kriya Yoga, Raja Yoga or Brahma Vidya are all the same. This is the greatest of all Yoga since this is the only Yoga which can dissolve our individual soul (Jivatma) with the Universal Soul (Paramatma) and can give salvation. Before dissolving with the Almighty, our soul should become so pure, just like the Universal Soul. Otherwise it cannot get mixed together, as oil and water cannot be mixed together. Only oil mixes with oil and water mixes with water. We must become just as pure as the Almighty in order to merge with Him.

Stages of Kriya Yoga

The Sadhana of a Kriya Yogi moves through different stages, out of which three stages are most important:

First Stage: This stage starts after Kriya Diksha (initiation) and continues until the subtle life force reaches the entrance/door of Sushumna. This is a very restless stage. In this stage, the Sadhak should have blind faith in the Guru and practice Kriya, always keeping the mind focused at Kutastha as per His guidance and instruction.

Second Stage: Mind becomes calm with the practice of Kriya. In this condition, the Sadhak tries to enter Sushumna with a calm mind. At that time, whatever happens in the physical body as well as the feelings that comes to the mind get reflected in Kutastha. Written instructions to the practitioner are shown with light rays that get flashed in the Kutastha. It is felt that somebody is telling you something within a split second and this is so powerful that it leaves a permanent impression on the mind. The Kriyaban will get a reply to all his queries and different types of sounds are heard which makes the Sadhak totally astonished.

After this, the **third stage** of Kriya starts. In the second stage, with Kriya practice, life force moves upward along the spine in the Sushumna. In this condition, awareness of the body is lost, and a type of Samadhi is experienced. But in the beginning, this lasts only for a short duration and the old samskaras (mind impressions) attack the Sadhak and bring him back down to the outward materialistic senses. In this stage, the Sadhak should control his mind and go on practicing Kriya. He should avoid having a mind busy in materialistic thoughts.

When the Sadhaka reaches the entrance of Sushumna, he sees the undisturbed and stable Divine light of Kutastha and this has a magnetic effect which attracts the mind. The gaze becomes fully fixed there, and in this condition the eyes do not blink or move. The body becomes fixed without any sensation.

Though the gaze becomes fixed, the mind of the Sadhaka still gets distracted because his thirst for materialistic pleasure still exists. In this condition, both the state of fixing the gaze at Kutastha and coming back to materialistic pleasure continues.

Samadhi or Yoga Nidra: During Kriya practice, at some point, a state similar to sleep is experienced. It is one of two types. One is the sleep of ignorance which comes because the mind gets tired from continuously having materialistic thoughts. But the state of sleep which comes out of Divine knowledge is a state of full lighted awareness, and the mind stays undisturbed in this state. This state of undisturbed mind, where materialistic thought has totally vanished, is a state of complete rest for the mind. This is the state of Samadhi. In this condition, the power comes to control the five outward sense organs. After doing pranayama, and you sit for meditation, sometimes it is very deep. You will feel sleepy, but not like a regular sleep where you lose awareness. This is a type of Samadhi. Nidra means sleep. Yoga nidra is sleeping, but also getting all knowledge, because you are entering the sushumna and going up. It is not a normal materialistic sleep, and you retain consciousness, despite feeling like you are going to sleep.

In the beginning, it is common for the Kriyaban (practitioner) to get frustrated and depressed because he has to sacrifice all the materialistic pleasures of life. He thinks that by doing Kriya, he is able to advance in the spiritual path but on the other hand, he is sacrificing the materialistic pleasures of life which are dearer to the mind. He feels it is better to get involved in materialistic life rather than doing Kriya. He feels that other people are enjoying and he is unnecessarily sacrificing materialistic pleasures. He feels that it is better to die than to suffer and achieve salvation. It is a suffering to both body and mind. Such a feeling may come at the beginning stage of Sadhana. The stage is comparable with a small snake swallowing a big frog. Neither the snake is able to swallow the frog nor is it able to throw it out. At this time, the mind dwells between good thoughts and bad thoughts. Mind wants to enjoy both Yoga & materialistic pleasure. This is not possible. One cannot cross a river keeping his feet separately in two boats. It will not lead to success. If we want to get out of the cycle of birth and death, we have to practice Yoga. At the beginning, one has to struggle much but after that, the state achieved is the state of continuous bliss.

Kriya of Sahasrasar Chakra

After completing Kriya in the six chakras, the Kriya of Sahasrasar Chakra begins; that is, Dharana, Dhyan and Samadhi.

Until and unless you get Siddhi (success) in Pratyahar, we are not eligible to do Dharana, Dhyan and Samadhi. What happens to us after we get success in Pratyahar is very difficult to express. Even though it cannot be easily expressed, a Kriya Practitioner experiences the steps within himself.

After success in Pratyahar, the Kriya of Dharana begins. This can be considered the second stage of meditation. In Dharana, a Kriya Practitioner gets the power to concentrate on a single point. After piercing Agna Chakra, you reach Kutastha, which is inside Agna. So, after piercing Agna you will find Kutastha there. From Kutastha, you will see this place for Dharana - a triangle, as in the diagram on the next page. At this point, you need to concentrate on each point of the triangle. Then you get the full knowledge - divine knowledge. Then, we have to concentrate on Sree Bindu which is in the center of the triangle. You have to go through Sree Bindu to reach Mula chakra. Nirvikalpa samadhi comes after piercing Sree Bindu.

So, if we watch until the end of Sahasrasar Chakra, this place which comes in our vision are the places of Dharana

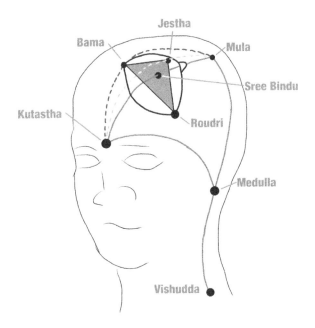

seen in this triangle. If we concentrate on those visible places, we get different types of knowledge and powers. (again, after reaching kutastha, you get this vision - which is after piercing agna).

The first place for Dharana is the Kutastha Bindu (star). The second place for Dharana is the Bama Bindu, as shown in the diagram, which is on the left side of the triangle in Sahasrasar Chakra. That is the area of intellect. Here we get the knowledge or ability to judge what is good and what is bad. Here we get the knowledge of pure intellect so that no evil thing can distort our mind. To understand this, we must know about desire. There are three things which create desire in the mind: the senses, the mind, and intellect. Therefore, until we cross the area of intellect, the last stage of desire persists, that is, attraction towards the body. The third stage of Dharana is the other corner of the triangle: "Roudri". This is the area of ego. So, here all egos get diminished (ended) and the wish to meet God increases and reaches the "Jestha" bindu.

This is the fourth stage of Dharana: Jestha, or the upper corner of the triangle. It is also the Chitta, or the store of all thoughts. This is the place where materialistic desire can't reach - only divine desire exists. After we completely overcome the negative desires of materialistic desire, we come very close to God, and God appears as a well wisher and a friend, and welcomes us and takes us in his lap.

The last stage of Dharana is Sree Bindu; that is, the center of Sahasrasar Chakra. From there, we move towards "Mula" Chakra with the power of Dhyan. This is the final stage of meditation and after piercing Mula Chakra we get total salvation. Regardless of how you think of this or say it, this means becoming absorbed in God or the Almighty.

This is the Kriya of Sahasrasar, which can't be understood by mere reading. If we want to realize this, we have to reach that stage and experience this directly, by ourselves.

Volume II

In the next volume of this series, more details on advanced practices are given, as well as Second, Third, and Fourth Kriya. Detailed explanations of the different types of Samadhi are given, as are a detailed account of the 18 egos we must get rid of in order to achieve salvation. Also, some stories about the lineage and myself are given at the end of Volume II. Volume II is considerably longer than this volume, which was limited to the essential practices and explanations. Remember - revered Lahiri Mahasaya said everything is possible with First Kriya.

Volume II will be published and made available at the same time as Volume I, but I am also planning to write and publish more advanced information later this year, 2017, in another book. Lastly, a contact email to reach some disciples I have permitted to give initiation will be provided in Volume II. As this lineage of Kriya is not affiliated with any formal organization, the only way to ensure its continuation is person-to-person through empowered disciples.

Glossary of Terms

Bhramari Guha - It is the divine tunnel inside which God exists

Bindu - Bright star

Bramharandhra - Is behind Sree Bindu, where both ends of Sushumna meet

Brahmananda - Internal Bliss

Celibacy - It gives power for deep meditation and for piercing the chakras to get knowledge in Sahasrasar via extremely subtle vision

Demons - Animality which are stored in our chitta - like sex, greed and anger, restlessness, etc

Dharana - 2nd stage of meditation. Focusing of attention on a particular object

Dhyan - 3rd stage of meditation. The deepest stage of meditation

Ganges - The holy river in India

Ida Nadi - Channel through which we breath

Japa - Chant

Kriyaban - Kriya Practitioner

Moksha - Type of salvation, but where duality still exists

Naad - Sounds

Nadi - Channels

Pingala Nadi - Channel through which we breath

Prana - Life force

Pratyahar - 1st stage of meditation - here self realization occurs

Sadhak - Yogi

Sadhana - To perform Kriya

Sahasrasar - Thousand petaled lotus in the top of the brain

Sanyas - A yogi who has completed all stages in Kriya (mainly, Kriya of the action area)

Sat Guru - realized guru

Satya, Rajo, Tamo - Three kinds of effects on the mind

Siddha - Realized

Siddhi - Spiritual Powers

Sushumna - The main channel through which we have to travel to reach Sahasrasar to get salvation. Only with extremely subtle Prana can we enter this channel

Vibhuti - Accord powers

Yogaruhra - Samadhi

Made in the USA
Coppell, TX
24 July 2021

59403574R10042